SHE GOT UP!

One woman's true-life
Testimony of how
"She Got Up"

JANICE
FREEMAN

She Got Up!
By Janice Freeman
Copyright: November, 2017

ISBN-13: 978-1979852586
ISBN-10: 1979852588

SOV Books
P.O. Box 2711
Downey, CA 90242
www.saintsofvalue.org

Printed in the United States of America

All scripture reference is derived from the King James and/or New American Standard Versions of the Bible.

Be sure to pick up a copy of Janice's first book!

A superb 4-star beginning.
The Vienna Schilling Review

The

URBAN HEART

Freeman writes with
piercing depth.
Editor, Stanton Book Company

The essential poetry collection of

JANICE
FREEMAN

Sublime poetry, rhythm and introspection.

Meet the Author ...

Janice Freeman is the: founder, president and CEO of *Catch the Change, Inc.--Catching the Vision of Someone Else's Dreams. Catch the Change (CTC),* is a non-profit, community-based organization focused on foster children and at-risk youth, ages 8 to 19 in Southern California. CTC's mission is to inspire and cultivate the necessary changes that positively impact the lives of youth; educationally, vocationally, and holistically. CTC utilizes a holistic approach to enhance academic improvement and success. Ms. Freeman is also a pastor, author, business owner, clothing designer, motivational speaker, mentor, Life Skill Coach and manager. As such, Ms. Freeman is a hard-working entrepreneur who regularly burns the midnight oil of achievement. Today, Janice Freeman resides in Southern California with her three sons, Joshua, Brandon, and Marcus. In her spare time, she enjoys writing poignant, introspective poetry, and most recently, writing her astounding memoir.

To every female who believes
She can get up!
To my Lord and Savior, Jesus Christ, whose
strength made it possible for me to get up!
To my mother, Shirley Freeman
My father, Webbie Freeman
And my sons, Joshua, Brandon and Marcus
For their support, encouragement and love!
Thank you and God bless.

Table of Contents

Introduction

Many times, we talk about how we got started and where we ended up. But there's not a lot of sharing concerning the actual "process" of getting out of certain situations.

In this book, I will share "how" I got out of different situations. The Lord placed it on my heart to write *She Got Up!* in order to share the different events that took place in my life and what process I used to get through them. I've been asked many questions like, "What did you do? How did you get out of that? Can you give me advice?"

I hope that what I share in this book will help many others. We all know that life's events happen to all of us. I want people to know they too can get up from any situation.

Everyone's circumstance is different. Ask yourself this question: Can I get up? I couldn't get up by myself. I had help getting up! I made up my mind and heart that I wasn't going to stay down. I had to get up! I can remember a time when the Lord whispered to me, "Get up and WIN!"

I wanted to be obedient to the Lord and share these experiences which, hopefully, will help someone else through their journey.

God bless you!

Janice Freeman

Philippians 4:13
"I can do all things through Christ
who strengthens me."

Heavenly Father,

Thank you for blessing me with a life of joy, peace and happiness. I thank you for allowing me to go through this journey of events that made me stronger, wiser and filled me with great understanding and love. Thank you for being with me and seeing me through it all. 1 Corinthians 15:57: "Thanks be to God, who gives us the victory through our Lord Jesus Christ."

Chapter 1

Unexpected Impact

The unexpected impact took place on October 8, 2009, while I was at work. I went to work that morning feeling good and happy.

I was a marketing specialist at a large, home supply store and it was a good, well-paying job, located only five minutes from my house. Life was good and my boys and I had all we needed. That morning, as always, I was excited to be at work with my co-workers and customers.

My supervisor gave me an assignment, to pull and reposition store products from shelves high above in the store. So, I grabbed our tall ladder, positioned it in front of the shelf, climbed up and began pulling the products. While doing so, the large, heavy advertising sign above me, fell and hit the top of my head. Immediately, I felt my neck jerk. When this happened, I held onto the rail to keep from falling and slowly stepped down the ladder. Upon reaching the floor, I collapsed. Leaning against the base of the shelf, I took several, slow, deep breaths. By then, I was experiencing a massive, painful headache. I looked around for co-workers, or someone to come but saw no one. Co-workers milled about constantly all over the store but on this day, there were none.

Finally, a co-worker saw me collapsed on the floor and helped me into a chair. She then escorted me to the restroom to wash my face. While in the restroom I whispered to God, "What happened just now?" In reply, God whispered back, "It was not your fault. It was the enemy!"

Shortly thereafter, my co-worker and I walked through the store to find our supervisor to inform her of what had just taken place. As I stood in front of the supervisor, I told her I wasn't feeling well.

Paramedics were called and I was transported to the hospital. I was examined by the ER doctor who took me off work for a few weeks with a sprained wrist and head contusion. I was tired, in a lot of pain, ready to go home and lay down.

Upon release from the hospital, I didn't have a way home, nor any money with me, so I asked the receptionist to help me get home. Just then, a man in the hospital lobby walked up and said, "I will take you home." But I heard the voice of God say, "You will not make it home." I told that guy very quickly, "No, thanks, that's OK," and I walked away from him. Then, a staff member came up to me and said I could "ask security for a card to call a cab." I informed them that I didn't have any money, that it was at home, but I took the card, anyway, and called the cab, whispering under my breath, "Lord help me get home safely. I need favor with the cab driver." Just then, a cab driver pulled up and said, "Did you call for a cab?"

I said, "Yes!"

He introduced himself and said, "I'm Solomon. I'll be your driver."

I informed him of my situation. "Solomon, can you take me home? I don't have money on me. I can pay you when we get to my place. Are you OK with that?" And he agreed.

When we arrived at my home, I started to step out of the cab to get his money, when suddenly, Solomon said, "That's OK. Take care of yourself," holding up his hand to stop the payment. "If you need anything, my wife and I can help you."

I thanked him and praised God for His favor as I watched Solomon drive away. During my three weeks at home, I found it odd that no one from my work called to see how I was.

Ever since then, I've suffered issues with my neck, back, head and wrist from this unexpected impact back in 2009. In the weeks ensuing, I had problems driving and doing other simple things we take for granted every day, and it was very challenging because I was in a lot of pain. So, I asked the Lord, "Who can I call to help me? I need help getting to my doctor's appointment." And the Lord said, "Solomon." I asked, the Lord. "When should I call?" and He said, "Now!"

Chapter 2

Homeless

In 2009, I purchased a beautiful, spacious, five-bedroom house in Palmdale. My youngest son attended school conveniently across the street. My second-oldest son attended school down the street.

As discussed earlier, I was working full-time as a marketing specialist just five minutes from my house. I was the sole bread-winner in our little family and for quite a while, things were going very well for us. It was suburban heaven!

I was also in the early stages of opening my own business, and just started operating my new ministry, *Talk 2 God 1st Ministries*. Things were going really well and I was excited about what

God was doing in my life, when the unexpected impact happened, recounted in the prior chapter.

Since October, 2009, I've had to undergo four neck and back surgeries. The first surgery took place six months after the accident, in March of 2010; the second one a month later, in April of 2010, the third in February, 2011, and the fourth in June of 2012.

I was a single mother raising my sons. My oldest son was living on his own and my two younger sons lived with me at the time of my injury. I called out to God to help me. I was in so much pain I couldn't move! Through the years of pain and suffering, I never once blamed God for anything that happened to me. Because of the surgeries and my inability to keep a steady job, my sons and I lost everything. Yes, everything---to the extent that my sons and I became homeless! I had lost all my income and I could barely move due to the injury.

Before long, I was getting letters coming to my house saying, "If you don't pay your mortgage you have to leave." So much was happening at once and I didn't have money for food, clothing, or shoes and school supplies for my sons. In fact, I couldn't pay for anything. I said, "God help me! I don't know what to do!"

During this time, Solomon, the cab driver, and I had stayed in touch on occasion. On my worst day, he called and asked if I needed anything? It was very embarrassing to ask him for help, but I eventually told him, "Yes. We need food."

I again reminded him that I didn't have any money, to which he once again replied, "That's OK. What do you and the boys like to eat?" Within a few short hours, Solomon and his wife brought us large bags of groceries. "This is my wife," said Solomon. "I've brought her to help you."

Solomon and his wife came through to help us on many occasions. He drove me to all my doctors' appointments in Palmdale, Los Angeles and Sherman Oaks, and surgeries at Cedar Sinai Hospital. While I was going through this process, I prayed to God daily, plus heard and read His word. I believed God would show up in my situation and followed His instructions to me, all day and every day. Through my pain, I praised God and asked Him to hold onto me, and not let me go. As I went in and out of the hospital, my body didn't feel like it would make it through, and yet I couldn't stop being a mother. It was very challenging--*but, God!* I asked for the strength and power of Jesus Himself.

One day, while I was in the hospital recovering from surgery, I had my Bible open but I couldn't read it at the time, because I couldn't lift up my arms. A nurse walked in and asked if she could read the Word to me. I responded in a soft voice, "Yes!" It was a blessing from God that the nurse read to me from the Word. I cried and I said, "Lord, thank you!"

Shortly thereafter, the nurse left the room and my brother, John Freeman, and his wife, Holly, came in and prayed for me and gave me encouraging words.

And now I'd like to share with you a situation that took place while I was dealing with the mortgage company. The staff at the mortgage company was not very nice, especially the head-guy over there. I was told this man would not work with anyone and that he was a real bulldog. When I was well enough, we met and I told him everything. As expected, he was really mean, and he kept saying, "No, no, no!" to everything. So, I went back home and prayed. (Pause for laughter.)

I told God everything that the mortgage man had said, and how badly he treated me. Three days later, God said, "Call a realtor." I said, "OK."

I prayed and asked God to guide me to the right realtor to help with my specific situation. In fact, I called a few realtors, listened to their marketing speeches and I knew that none of them were for me. The last call I made was to a realtor, by the name of Linda P. We spoke briefly and I knew the Lord had led me to her. We met, I gave her all the information and she helped put my house up for sale. Good things happened after that.

She had a conversation with the bulldog at the mortgage company while I prayed and gave thanks to God. I said, "God, I need his 'no' to be a 'yes' on everything we ask!" Then, Linda P. and I went to meet with him again, and we got everything we asked for! The Lord had turned the impossible 'no' into an astounding 'yes'!

There were also property taxes due on the property and the gentlemen said, "Don't worry about it, we'll pay for it on your behalf." Then he said, "Sign this contract agreement and it will not go on your credit report. Your credit report will read as if you never purchased the property, and now there's a zero balance."

I received no money from the sale of the house but my credit report remained intact, and I was released from the overwhelming debt, mounting interest charges and late fees!

From there, my sons and I moved in with friends and prepared to heal my body--and our lives in general.

I praised and gave God thanks for what He did on my behalf. By following the instructions of God and communicating with Him every moment, throughout the process, She Got Up! and moved on!

Chapter 3

Miracle Mile

In June of 2012, I received a voicemail from my doctor's office while attending my cousin's funeral. "Janice, please call your doctor A.S.A.P.! We have to do an emergency surgery."

I called them back and said, "What? I thought I was done with surgeries!"

The doctor had reviewed my x-rays and found that the stimulator, a medical implant which helped to dull the pain, had become unattached!

"Yes, I'm sorry, but we have to go back in and reattach it." I was dumb-founded!

Right after this was brought to my attention, my body felt weird; as though something was going to bust wide open. I went into prayer, hurt and disappointed; it was an inexplicable feeling.

I said, "God, I don't want to keep going through this. It seems like I'm having surgeries every year! Can you help me?" I was crying by then. I didn't want to go through another surgery, and I was not happy with my doctors.

I didn't feel like being around other people at the time because of what I was dealing with. I continued in prayer, "God, I don't know if my body can handle another neck and back surgery!" Then I asked the Lord, "Do you want me to have it replaced or not put back in at all?"

The Lord said, "Fast for three days and meditate on Malachi 4:2."

Malachi 4:2
"But unto you that fear My name,
shall the Sun of Righteousness arise
with healing in His wings…"

During the three-day fast, I repeated, "Jesus, arise over my life with healing in your wings," over and over. And then, the Lord spoke…

The Lord said, "Take it out." And I said, "Lord, you know that I'm not able to use my arms without this device. If you want me to take the device out, I need you to make my arms and hands functional, as though I was created before the foundation of the world!" It was a tall order but it had to be said.

During my three-day fast, the Lord gave me a prophetic dream. He showed me "the name" of the Ortho-surgeon who was to perform my surgery, even though I had never met him, nor heard of him. Still in the dream, I also saw the name of the clinic---*Miracle Mile Hospital*---and the actual names of his assistants---*Anna and George!*

When I arrived at the appointment, every name in my dream was confirmed. As I drove up, I saw the *Miracle Mile Hospital,* and I said, "I see you, God. Thank you for the confirmation." And of course, I met his assistants, Anna and George!

I had the surgery at the Miracle Mile Hospital. After the surgery, I was laying in the recovery room, resting, when the Ortho-surgeon came in. He had just returned from a wedding and was still wearing his smart-looking tuxedo.

"I usually don't visit my patients at night. Are you a Christian?" he asked.

I said, "Yes; why?"

"I felt something different in my hand while I was operating on you," he said, quizzically.

And I said to myself, *That's God!*

"I had to come in and ask you," he continued. "Can I put your neck photo into my surgery book?" The book was filled with before and after X-rays. "It's a perfect photo and I'd really like to include it."

I told him he could. During this conversation, the surgeon told me his entire medical unit was filled with Believers in Christ!

After the surgery, I was able to move my arms and hands freely "without" the implanted device! Hallelujah! She Got Up! after being down so long! She trusted God with the instructions He gave her and she was healed. She trusted God for her to rise!

Although my body had been mended, my exterior life was still in shambles. I and my sons were still homeless and staying with friends.

Three weeks after this surgery, I spoke to a friend of mine who stated she had a friend, who was married with children, and that she would let us stay with her family, until I was able to get back on my feet. They were (and still are) a very nice, Christian family.

My friend asked me to call and speak to the lady and her husband so I called them the following day. We set a date and time to meet at their house and my friend, who made the connection, came with me.

The meeting was *so anointed*, I was able to move in the next day! This was in July of 2012. They asked how much time I'd need and I told them until January of the next year; a good six months. I was in post-surgery pain and they gave us one of their spare rooms. My sons and I stayed in the room together and we were grateful for the shelter.

Chapter 4

The Supernatural School

The new school year was upon us and I had to get my son registered for school, so, we took a taxi to the school district. I was still in pain, wearing a neck brace and walking with a walker for balance.

Every step I took I wanted to sit down but, I had to keep going. I was trying to get my sons into a particular school district, but the staff gave me the run-around, which was challenging, to say the least.

So, I went back to the place I was staying at, and went into prayer. I said, "God, your will be done regarding the school you want my son to attend, and I ask for favor in this. In Jesus' name, amen!"

I went back and forth with the school district staff and on the third time, the Superintendent said, "OK, I will give your sons a permit for one year, but you'll have to come back every year, until they graduate to renew the permit."

Again, this was the Lord answering my persistent prayer.

At the end of the first year, I went back to the Superintendent and she said, "Mrs. Freeman, you don't have to come back every year. I'm going to give you the permit for the full four years, so you won't have to keep coming back. I wish you and your son all the best."

I was told from another party they don't ever do that in this district, and I replied, "Well, God approved it for me!" She Got Up! to get her son into the school of God's choice.

Chapter 5

Get Up and Win!

During this time, I was still walking around with that walker and the neck-brace on and the doctor said I should be in the bed. But I had to push on and trust God. I couldn't stop now after all these obstacles and challenges. I had to keep going, not just for myself but for my family. I was communicating with God daily, moment by moment, asking for His guidance.

As you go through the process, God will give you favor and send help your way. God is there no matter what you go through. He sees your tears, He knows your pain, He understands your fall, when no one else does--and He knows how to raise you up! Believe, trust and have faith. He will help you through the process. Don't give in and don't give up! It's too easy to give up! When you push, do so with faith, knowing God is with you, holding you up. Continue to worship and praise God through it all! You may feel like you don't want to keep going but remember: Jesus went to the cross for us. Jesus took everything that we are going through, or have gone through, right to the cross.

I asked God to help me understand my journey. "Is this fall for my purpose and destiny? Or is this an empty fall?" Because of the love God has for me, I heard him say, "Get Up and Win!"

It was the whisper of love. That whisper motivated, inspired and pushed me in the direction I needed to go, with grace and mercy. Stay in the Word while you're going through the valley. Trust God throughout your journey. When so many things were happening to me all at once, I saw myself in the middle of the boxing-ring, getting hit, blow after blow. I'm still standing and wobbling but I didn't fall. God held me up!

He said, "You're going to stand through this!" It made me a stronger and better warrior. I got up from the hits of the enemy and conquered my situation, to where I'm now able to see and hear Him clearly!

Chapter 6

Is It Worth The Ring?

Being married is supposed to be a beautiful union. I was married to a man I met in Long Beach, California. We had a great time together and he was respectful, kind and beautiful. He was in the military, born and raised in Texas, and we transferred to his hometown.

When we got to Texas, everything changed. He got together with some of his old buddies and they were hanging out and drinking. One night, he again wanted to go out and I said, "OK, enjoy your night out with your friends."

The following day he again went out to party with this friends, but he failed to leave me any money for groceries and other things we needed for the house. I had two young children at the time and was pregnant with my third. I had to walk "miles" to the store with a baby on my hip, one walking along the road with me, and one on the way. My husband and I had gone to the doctor together at one point, whereupon the doctor told both of us that mine was a high-risk pregnancy.

Two days later, he came home and said, "Go out there and clean the car." But he knew I wasn't supposed to do that because of the pregnancy but at that moment, I felt that I had to clean the car, or he would leave again—so I cleaned the car.

One night he called me at two in the morning. He was in jail and asked me to bail him out. I said, "I don't have the money to get you out." He got mad and said, "Call my grandfather for the money." I did so, and his grandfather posted bail. Then, he came home like nothing ever happened.

Don't get me wrong; we did have some good times together. When he came home from jail I noticed he didn't have his wedding ring on. I asked him about it and he said the guard at the jail didn't give it back to him. That wasn't settled with my spirit. He lied to me about that. A week later, he wanted to go out again and he asked me for his wallet. I told him I didn't know where it was. So, he hit me, but I still couldn't tell him where it was, because I had no idea.

After he left with his friends, I went to my neighbor's house next door and told her what had happened. She called the military police on base and reported the assault. When he arrived home, he was drunk and sleepy and passed out in bed. Then, came the knock on the door. It was the military police. They took him to a certain location on base and he made the choice to never come back to the house, nor our marriage.

I was kicked out of base housing with two children while pregnant, and we slept in my car, in the park and at different people's homes. My husband at the time didn't want me to work, so I had no money of my own.

I hired a divorce attorney who told me to stay in town until the divorce was final. So, I sent my children to my parents' house in California while I looked for work. It was very challenging. Thankfully, I found work as a CNA (Certified Nurse's Assistant) and cook at the county jail. Shortly thereafter, I ran into my ex-husband, whereupon he felt the need to tell me that he had slept with all of his female friends, at work and at their place.

I was so incensed by this, that I went out to the pier and thought about jumping. I felt ashamed and defeated because my marriage failed. I was bitter, angry, hurt, lost, and I didn't know how to face my family. Then, still on the pier, I heard a female's voice call out my name. "Janice! What are you doing?" I didn't answer her but she kept calling my name and eventually, she caught up to me. No one knew I was there, but God! He sent her over to me so I wouldn't end my life. She was one of the military wives; a caring, good person.

I worked until I had enough money to pay my attorney and a bus ticket back home. I prayed for God's protection through it all, as did my friend, the military wife. I left everything to him, got on that greyhound bus and never looked back. She Got Up! to start over with her children.

Chapter 7

The Fake God-Man

It's now 2013, and I was safely back in California, in my parents' cozy, Long Beach house. What would I have done without them?

I rested for a good six months and slowly began looking for work. Eventually, I got a well-paying job and my sons and I were once again able to rent our own place.

That year, I was out and about with some friends, shopping, when we ran into a gentleman whom I knew and was interested in, from a long time ago. The gentlemen had an interest toward me as well, so we exchanged phone numbers, began talking and seeing each other.

We engaged in great conversations and one day, I invited him over for lunch. Before long, we became a couple. We went to church together, talked about God and prayed together, which soon turned into daily events.

Then one day, he started acting aggressively and asking me for money, which was a shocker. More often than not, I had to turn my head, so he wouldn't see my facial expressions. It was a good thing that we lived separately.

Time went on and more untoward things about him began to unfold. Days, weeks, months and almost a year went by and his behavior set me on edge. I didn't know what to do, so I said, "Lord, help me get out of this."

I had strong feelings for this man and I wanted it to work. I kept hoping he would change now that God was in his life. One day, he was over at my place and he again asked me for money. I said no, and that's when he slapped me, pushed me against the wall and twisted my arm to where he almost broke it. I went to the hospital that same day, whereupon the doctor asked me what had happened. I told him I had fallen. The doctor said my arm was sprained, he wrapped it and gave me pain medicine.

The man continued to ask me for money and if I didn't give it to him, he kept hitting me. Now, mind you, I had sons and brothers (still do), who would've handled this guy, but I didn't want them to get involved, or in trouble with the law.

I experienced physical, emotional and verbal abuse under this guy. Although he shattered my self-esteem and I became very depressed, I was determined to get him out of my life. This guy had to go!

When I looked in the mirror, a broken woman stared back at me. And that was it. I needed to pick up the pieces. I wanted my life back, past all the verbal and physical abuse, past all the drama and pain. I would have to pack up and leave that crazy situation because the enemy was trying to kill me.

"I'm going to take my life back!" I determined. "Everything! My peace and joy, my mind and self-esteem, boldness and strength! I have to get back on track and love me!"

Chapter 8

Picking Up The Pieces

As I had always done in the past, I prayed; this time, to get that man out of my life. "Lord, I need your help to get out of this."

The Lord said, "Get some boxes and start packing." So, I went to get boxes and told the boys we were moving.

I had a dream a few days later. In the dream, this man was wearing a certain type of clothing and I saw exactly how he was going to act and what he would say.

Later that evening, he showed up at my door, and it all played out, exactly as I saw in the dream, right down to the clothes he wore and things he said. I was laying on the couch in the living room and he peered through the curtained window.

He called out, "Janice, I see you! Open the door!" I was by myself and scared. I didn't move for a long time. In my mind, I was talking to God. "Lord, what should I do?"

Strangely, the Lord said, "Open the door for him."

I said, "God, what do I tell him? He's gonna' see these boxes!"

God said, "Tell him you are moving downstairs to a lower unit that is better for you."

So, reluctantly, I walked over to the door and opened it. Sure enough, he asked me what the boxes were for and where I was going. Then, he checked my whole house to make sure I didn't have another man hidden in one of the rooms.

Finally, I said, "Can you please leave? There's no one else here!" Getting him to leave took ten minutes, which seemed like an hour.

The following day was Saturday and I walked to the U-Haul. It took me an hour and half to walk there, because my sons had taken the car out of town. I rented the U-Haul truck, drove it back to my place and packed everything in that truck in less than three hours! I didn't know I could move that fast! I was trying to get out of there before the Fake God-Man came back.

My sons were out of town and when they got home, they saw the truck filled with our things and I said, "Let's go!" I left and never went back.

God told me in no uncertain terms, if I hadn't gotten out of that relationship, he would have killed me. She Got Up! by picking up the broken pieces!

Chapter 9

Forgiven Fall

One day, I was struggling with the sins of my past. They seemed to come back to taunt me and make me feel guilty. I prayed and asked God for forgiveness for all my fallen sins. Soon after that, I was riding the Metro Link from Palmdale to Los Angeles. On the Metro, I heard the voice of the Lord say, "Your divorce is final."

I replied, "I'm not married."

He said, "Your divorce from the men you have been with in the past."

I was puzzled by this word. Then, I realized what the Lord meant. From that moment forward, I was free from my past sins. God forgave me because of His great love for me.

Treasure You ...

Treasure your worth...
Treasure your value...
Treasure your motherhood...

Treasure your heart...
Treasure your mind...
Treasure your abilities...
Treasure your character...

Treasure your walk...
Treasure your beauty...
Treasure your love...
Treasure your smile...

Treasure your confidence...

Treasure your uniqueness...

Treasure your destiny...

Treasure your dreams...

Treasure your purpose...

Treasure your life...

Treasure your singleness...

Treasure your gifts...

Treasure your voice...

Treasure You!

(c) 05/12/2012

Chapter 10

Treasure You

I was operating within other people's identities, and didn't realize those were false. For instance, I would like the way someone did their hair, and I'd set about to get that same hairstyle. But if the hairstylist didn't do it exactly the way I wanted it done, I'd get mad at the stylist.

Or, I'd see someone's personality traits and try to copy them. And, of course, that didn't work either and it didn't last longer than a week. Then, I tried putting on my make-up like a friend of mine, but when I looked in the mirror, I was hurt because it didn't look like hers. I remember taking it off and feeling ugly.

I also shopped and wore things, like my friends. Their clothes flowed so nicely on them, but when I glanced in the mirror, I didn't like what I saw.

I tried doing different things to be a different person. I was not happy. I was dealing with self-esteem issues. I had an attitude because I wasn't comfortable with myself. I had issues that I had to deal with quickly, because people didn't want to be around me. They'd say, "You're not yourself. Stop trying to be like other people!"

So, I had to stop and be still. I went to see my brother, John, and told him what was going on with me. He said, "Sister, I love you and you know I'm gonna' to tell you the truth, in love, because, I love you!" When tears flowed down my face, he said, "It's OK to cry."

He said, "You have to love Janice! You have to find out who Janice really is! Take some time to look in the mirror and *really look at yourself.* Look at the beautiful young lady God created. Everything about you is beautiful!"

He continued, "You have to believe it for yourself. I know it doesn't feel good, but you have to do this for you and your sons," he continued. "What do you want your sons to see and say about their mother? Janice, you have a lot to offer, but offer it to yourself first!" Then, my brother took me through an exercise.

"Start saying this while you're looking at yourself in the mirror. I love Janice. I love my smile. I love my hair. I love my ears. I love my mouth. I love the size of my head. I love my size. I love my body. I love who God created me to be. I am beautiful. I am bold. I am confident. I love myself. I am blessed. I am strong. I am a visionary. I am fearfully and wonderfully made. I am more than a conqueror. I'm an overcomer. I am transformed by the renewing of my mind. I am victorious through Christ."

And so, I spoke these things over myself every day, and still do. Speaking these things had a profound effect on me. Today, I love me! It took time for me to get there, but I am here now.

I want to thank God for my brother, John Freeman. Thank you for your counsel and prayers. God bless you, my dear brother!

SHE GOT UP!

She has a non-profit organization:
Catch The Change, Inc.
*Catching The Vision Of
Someone Else's Dream.*

Catch The Change works with youth,
conducting inspiring, life-changing
workshops around Southern California.

In Closing

I was raised by my parents, a strong husband and wife team, the loving father and mother, whom I love dearly. They raised me up in the Word of God. As an adult, I stepped away from my Heavenly Father, momentarily, to do whatever I wanted. My parents prayed and never ceased to keep me before God. My parents had eleven children. I thank God for my entire family!

Judged By The Fall

There was a time when I recall
Falling into sin
I fell in the flesh before marriage
And my heart grew dim
I was judged for the fall
With my soon-to-be husband
Before I reached the altar
It came to an end
I was talked about badly
By a person called friend
Made me feel real' bad
And ashamed of the fall
I was scheduled to be married
And before I said, I do
My friend fussed at me and said
I didn't deserve it, at all
"What kind of person are you?
You're not a lady!" she said
I got an ear full from her
Yes, I felt bad too
So I repented and asked God
To forgive me

She didn't know that, I didn't tell her
God is a forgiving God
He doesn't make you feel bad
God didn't judge me
He loves me happy or sad
He knew I made a mistake!
He said, do not judge one another
Romans 3:23: "For all have sinned
And come short of glory …"
Your fall may be different
From another one's story
So don't beat them and judge them
For their weakness and mayhem
Why not pray for their struggle?
What caused their fall, their attitude?
We have to be real
Proverbs 24:16: "For a just man falls
Seven times and rises again!"
You don't know why, how or when
This is what I want to tell you…
Get up from the fall!
Don't stay in it!
SHE GOT UP!

Soul Food

Psalms 1

1 Blessed is the man who does not walk in the counsel of the wicked nor stands with sinners, nor sits in the seat of mockers.

2 But his delight is in the law of the LORD, and on his law he meditates day and night.

3 He is like a tree planted by streams of water, which yields its fruit in season and whose leaf does not wither. Whatever he does prospers.

4 Not so, the wicked! They are like chaff that the wind blows away.

5 Therefore the wicked will not stand in the judgment, nor sinners in the assembly of the righteous.

6 For the LORD watches over the way of the righteous, but the way of the wicked will perish.

Psalms 23

A Psalm of David.

1 The LORD is my shepherd, I shall not be in want.

2 He makes me lie down in green pastures, he leads me beside quiet waters.

3 He restores my soul. He guides me in paths of righteousness for his name's sake.

4 Even though I walk through the valley of the shadow of death, I will fear no evil, for you are with me. Your rod and your staff, they comfort me.

5 You prepare a table before me in the presence of my enemies. You anoint my head with oil; my cup overflows.

6 Surely goodness and love will follow me all the days of my life, and I will dwell in the house of the LORD forever.

Psalms 91

1 He who dwells in the shelter of the Most High will rest in the shadow of the Almighty.

2 I will say of the LORD, "He is my refuge and my fortress, my God, in whom I trust."

3 Surely he will save you from the trapper's snare and from the deadly pestilence.

4 He will cover you with his feathers, and under his wings you will find refuge; his faithfulness will be your shield and rampart.

5 You will not fear the terror of night, nor the arrow that flies by day,

6 nor the pestilence that stalks in the darkness, nor the plague that destroys at midday.

7 A thousand may fall at your side, ten thousand at your right hand, but it will not come near you.

8 You will only observe with your eyes and see the punishment of the wicked.

9 If you make the Most High your dwelling--even the LORD, who is my refuge --

10 then no harm will befall you, no disaster will come near your tent.

11 For he will command his angels concerning you, to guard you in all your ways;

12 they will lift you up in their hands, so that you will not strike your foot against a stone.

13 You will tread upon [kings and rulers] the lion and the cobra; you will trample the great lion and the serpent.

And then the Lord answered …

14 "Because you love me," says the LORD, "I will rescue you. I will protect you because you have acknowledged my name.

15 You will call upon me, and I will answer you; I will be with you in trouble, I will deliver you and honor you.

16 With long life will I satisfy you and show you my salvation."

Prayer of Salvation

Father, your word says, that if I confess with my mouth that Jesus is Lord, and I believe in my heart that You have raised Him from the dead, I shall be saved.

Father, I confess that Jesus is my Lord.

I make Him Lord of my life, right now.

I believe in my heart that You raised Jesus from the dead.

I thank you for forgiving me for all my sin.

Jesus is now my Lord, and I am a new creation in Christ Jesus.

Amen.

Acknowledgements

First and foremost, I would like to thank God for being the greatest gift in my life. I would also like to thank my children for standing beside me throughout my career and writing this book. They have been my inspiration and motivation for continuing to improve my knowledge and moving forward in my career. And a special thanks to my family and friends. God bless you!

Janice Freeman

Webbie Freeman & Shirley Freeman
Rest In Peace
My dearest mother and father.
I Love You!

We hope you enjoyed the true-life, and certainly supernatural events, of Janice Freemen. To order more copies of this book, or to contact Ms. Freeman, write:

Janice Freeman
Catch The Change, Inc.
396 S. California Ave #35
West Covina, CA 91791
Email: catchthechange@yahoo.com

Made in the USA
Monee, IL
17 August 2023